1,003 Great Things About Moms

Other Books by Lisa Birnbach

1,003 Great Things About Teachers
1,003 Great Things About Friends
1,003 Great Things About Kids
1,003 Great Things About Getting Older
The Official Preppy Handbook
Lisa Birnbach College Books
Going to Work
Loose Lips

Other Books by Ann Hodgman

1,003 Great Things About Teachers
1,003 Great Things About Friends
1,003 Great Things About Kids
1,003 Great Things About Getting Older
My Baby-Sitter Is a Vampire (series)
Stinky Stanley (series)
Beat This!
Beat That!

Other Books by Patricia Marx

1,003 Great Things About Teachers
1,003 Great Things About Friends
1,003 Great Things About Kids
1,003 Great Things About Getting Older
How to Regain Your Virginity
You Can Never Go Wrong by Lying
Blockbuster
Now Everybody Really Hates Me
Now I Will Never Leave the Dinner Table
How to Survive Junior High
Meet My Staff

1,003
Great Things
About Moms

Lisa Birnbach • Ann Hodgman • Patricia Marx

**Andrews McMeel
Publishing**

Kansas City

1,003 Great Things About Moms

For information, write Andrews McMeel Publishing,
an Andrews McMeel Universal company,
4520 Main Street, Kansas City, Missouri 64111.

04 05 06 BIN 10 9 8 7 6 5 4 3

Library of Congress Cataloging-in-Publication Data
Birnbach, Lisa.
1,003 great things about moms / Lisa Birnbach, Ann
    Hodgman, Patricia Marx.
        p. cm.
ISBN 0-7407-2239-5
    1. Mothers—Humor. I. Title: One thousand and three
    great things about moms. II. Title: One thousand-three
    great things about moms. III. Hodgman, Ann. IV.
    Marx, Patricia. V. Title.

PN6231.M68 B57 2002
818'.5402—dc21   2001045704

Book design by Holly Camerlinck

Attention: Schools and Businesses

Andrews McMeel books are available at quantity discounts
with bulk purchase for educational, business, or sales
promotional use. For information, please write to:
Special Sales Department, Andrews McMeel Publishing,
4520 Main Street, Kansas City, Missouri 64111.

1,003 Great Things About Moms

Moms can give very fast baths.

They can whip together a
delicious dinner when there's
"absolutely nothing here to eat!!"

If absolutely necessary, Mom will wax your leg hair herself.

Who else would hold your chewed-up gum in her hand?

You have her eyes . . .

. . . And her tendency to gain weight in the derriere.

She'll buy you a toy when you're sick.

You'll never find a cheaper housekeeper.

Mother knows how old you have to be to cross the street without holding her hand.

Excellent critical abilities . . .
especially when it comes to you.

She remembers shockingly minute
and trivial details about the Trojan
War, just in time for your history
class's unit on ancient Greece.

She can still decline her Latin.

So what if Mom calls it
"new math"; it still works.

You're in her will.

She knows when you've been
good or bad, so be good for
goodness'. . . No, that's Santa . . .
No, come to think of it,
that's your mother.

She keeps your father company.

Don't worry—she'll take care
of Thanksgiving.

Somewhere, someplace, she has
your birth certificate . . . maybe.

You'll always look younger
than she does.

You can borrow her jewelry . . .

. . . And not return it.

Though she has a lot of dirt on you, she'd never blackmail you.

Name one other person who would sew name tags into your underwear.

She saves your letters from camp
because she believes someday they
will be valuable.

Mothers know when to give
you Tylenol, and when to
give you Motrin.

And when you need Advil.

Or Valium.

They understand you and
still love you.

She's your own personal laundress.

She still has her original recording
of *Abbey Road*, which is now worth
a lot of money.

She intends to give you her
snow-dome collection one day.

Mom allows you to criticize her
outfits without being insulted.

Mothers have soft upper arms.

When you cannot fall asleep,
she'll read you your
Frances book again.

When you really, annoyingly
refuse to sleep, she'll let you lie
down on a "nest" on the floor
of your bedroom.

Moms know thirteen
different ways to fold a napkin.

How We See Our
Moms When We're . . .

One day old:
a blur.

Two months old:
milk machine.

Three months old:
something to smile at.

Six months old:
something that pushes a spoon
in our face.

One year old:
a hand to hold while we
try to walk.

Two years old:
something that says no
all the time.

Three years old:
Daddy's ally.

Four years old:
bad-dream vanquisher.

Five years old:
role model.

Six years old:
expert French-braider.

Seven years old:
flash card coach.

Eight years old:
chauffeur.

Nine years old:
room cleaner-upper.

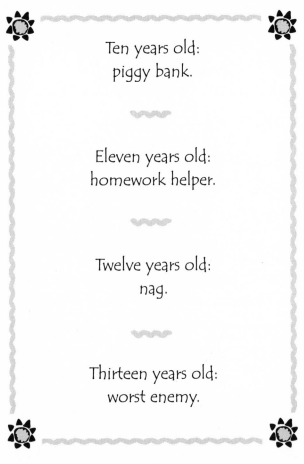

Ten years old:
piggy bank.

Eleven years old:
homework helper.

Twelve years old:
nag.

Thirteen years old:
worst enemy.

Fourteen years old:
source of shame.

Fifteen years old:
slave driver.

Sixteen years old:
clothing naysayer.

Seventeen years old:
non-car lender.

Eighteen years old:
college-selection sounding board.

Nineteen years old:
hypocrite.

Twenty years old:
"I've really changed at college"
sounding board.

Twenty-one years old:
career-choice sounding board.

Twenty-two years old:
housekeeper.

Twenty-three years old:
furniture storer.

Twenty-four years old:
apartment lease cosigner.

Twenty-five years old:
psychiatrist.

Twenty-eight years old:
psychiatrist-payer.

Thirty years old:
confidante.

Thirty-two years old:
baby-sitter for our children.

Forty years old:
friend.

Fifty years old:
font of wisdom.

Sixty-five years old:
beloved memory.

She never *doesn't* cry while watching
A Baby Story on the Learning
Channel.

Mom will take you to the
museum to see the new show.

Mothers really, really understand
the merits of Murphy's Oil Soap.

She knows a surprising amount
about Oprah and Stedman.

Believe it or not, Mommy was
once the best relief pitcher
at Wellesley.

She'll teach you how to
bake a challah.

A Mother's
Greatest Problems

Being nice to her child's friend
whom she hates.

Three-year-old's horrible candor
when she sees a man she thinks
is pregnant.

Five-year-old refuses to
kiss Grandpa.

Is it okay to pick your
toddler's nose?

Child unknowingly tracks
dog doo all over the house
before dinner party.

The vodka in the liquor cabinet
is mysteriously disappearing.

Ugly hand-me-downs
from her sister's kids.

Trying to avoid laughing
inappropriately during
the school play.

Trying to avoid crying
inappropriately during
the school concert.

Maternity clothes that are now
four years out of date.

Saying nice things about
her daughter's sonnet.

Swim practice at 5:00 A.M.

Kids who cut their own bangs.

Trigonometry homework.

Father says it's fine for kid to
stay out past curfew.

Refraining from pointing out
that her thirty-two-year-old
has put on a few pounds.

Her son announces he's naming
his son "Rover."

Her daughter gives up her
law practice to become
a Benedictine nun.

Her child asks for an advance
on Aunt Emily's will.

Being nice to her child's fiancé,
whom she hates.

Mom always carries your inhaler with her.

She is never without Benadryl.

Moms smell like moms.

She'll decide when you can ride your bike to school.

She doesn't mind if you bring
your laundry home from college.
In fact, she's kind of pleased.

Mothers spend their weekends
in service to you.

She's the best chauffeur you can
afford at age thirteen.

She doesn't get upset when you laugh at her dancing at the Bennetts' bar mitzvah.

She understands that the mother of the groom has to wear beige.

She'll finish scooping out your jack-o'-lantern if you get bored.

She almost got a tattoo when
she was your age, too.

Until she thought better of it.

According to her calculations
based on when she knew Sharon
Stone, Sharon Stone should
be almost fifty.

She can drink you under the table.

Come to Think of It, Mom Does Know Best

Silence of the Lambs really was too scary for you.

You did sprain your ankle wearing those platform sandals.

The girl whose mother let her wear whatever she wanted did end up in trouble.

You did lose your virginity
on that teen tour.

Your hair did grow back thicker,
darker, and coarser once you
started shaving.

You should have gone to that
girls' school after all.

Phillip *was* no good for you.

And you forgot about him as soon as you met Todd.

You did get addicted to cigarettes, even though they were just lites.

You did puke in Mrs. Miller's boxwood during the tea party.

You were a late bloomer after all.

She will cook dinner, clear the
table, and wash the dishes . . .
if you have an exam in
the morning.

Mom isn't devastated when you
decide to quit ballet. Or if she is,
she keeps it to herself.

Mothers never run out of stamps.

Mothers are rich enough to get
rolls of quarters at the bank.

They won't care if you're not
a finalist. Or a semifinalist.

To your mother,
you're always beautiful.

She was once a daughter, too.

When your dad says no,
your mom will say yes.

She still remembers *le subjonctif.*

She can fix your horrible perm
herself, or at least will pay for
someone else to do it.

She paid the postage for all those chain letters you sent out in eighth grade.

She walks your dog every night at midnight. God forbid you should offer to do it yourself.

Mothers know the right way to bleach your mustache.

She took an "easy A" music class
in her freshman year with the
host of *Survivor.*

Mom has the most beautiful linen
place mats, not that she'll lend
them to you.

Mothers are amazingly fast
at calculating tips.

Parenting Articles We'd Like to See

"Why You're a Better Parent Than Your Mom"

"Go Ahead! Spank Your Kids!"

"Ten Reasons It's Your Spouse's Fault"

"Why You Should Tell Your Neighbor She's a Bad Mom"

"Scientists Say Eating McDonald's Every Night Boosts Reading Skills"

"Toddlers Learn More When Parked in Front of the TV"

"Children Know Best When It Comes to Nutrition"

"Do-It-Yourself Projects
You Can Buy"

"Ten Mistakes It's Okay
to Make"

"Why a Baby-Sitter Is Better
Than You!"

"Violence on TV Got My Son into Yale"

"U.S. Presidents Who Got C's in High School"

"Video Games Linked to Fewer Ear Infections"

They seem to know every
opera libretto.
(See also under "Annoying.")

If you get a really important
phone call, your mother will
let you be late for dinner.

She thinks you need a warmer
winter coat, so she buys you one.

She didn't make you pay her back
for the Palm Pilot.

She got cable installed
at the cottage.

Mom never asks if *Sex and the City*
seems accurate to you, your own
single self.

Great Things About Grandmothers

Mom's rules don't apply
in her house.

She is thrilled to
buy your love.

She's willing to
play cards endlessly.

She's not afraid of spoiling you.

Florida condo!

Birthday checks.

Homemade chocolate-chip cookies.

Candy on the coffee table.

Life Savers in her pocketbook.

She never asks if you did your homework.

Knows all the dirt on your parents.

She's a knit-aholic.

Doesn't care if you spend all day
in chat rooms because she doesn't
even know what they are.

Likes your school photo even
though your eyes are closed.

She voted for President Kennedy!

She's willing to pick you up from school. And she always has candy in her car.

She has first editions of all the Beatrix Potter books.

She met Frank Sinatra in
Las Vegas when she was there
on her honeymoon.

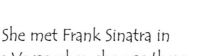

She met Wayne Newton in
Reno when she went there
for her divorce.

Her incredible skill with
phyllo dough.

Her hand stitching is as uniform as
a sewing machine's.

No curfew when you sleep
at her house.

She always ends a visit by pressing
a five-dollar bill in your hand,
as if she were tipping
the hairdresser.

Want her rhinestone ring?
Ask and it's yours.

She doesn't think it's gauche
to serve Jell-O.

On your last family vacation,
she got you a room that didn't
connect to hers.

She's just fine when you turn down
admission to her alma mater.

She still cooks nice meals for
your father after all the children
have moved out.

She buys ten tubes of Chap Stick
at a time and scatters them
throughout the house.

She let you become a vegetarian
although you don't like fish,
legumes, eggs, or vegetables.

Your mother doesn't mind if
you wear ridiculously tight
bell-bottoms to the family
reunion, or if she does,
she doesn't say so.

Mom's Rules in the Kitchen

No ketchup bottles on the table.

No adding salt until you've tasted the food.

No humming while eating.

No dessert without three bites
of your main course.

No kicking your sister
under the table.

No electronic equipment
at the table unless World War III
breaks out.

No complaining about the baby's table manners.

No building mountains out of mashed potatoes.

No pouring gravy "lava" over the mashed-potato mountains.

No complaining about your
day until Daddy's had a chance
to complain about his.

No TV during dinner,
even though everyone knows
it would improve the
family's mood 500 percent.

Mom's Rules
on Vacation

Smile and look like you're having
a good time in all photos.

Nobody back in the pool until at
least half an hour after you've
eaten (even though doctors no
longer believe this is necessary).

No fighting in the car
except for the parents.

Only pack what you
can carry yourself.

"Leaflets three, let it be."

Sunscreen, sunscreen, sunscreen.

Comic books are okay for
long car trips.

Excess candy is okay for
long car trips.

Don't make horrible faces at the people in other cars.

Always go to the bathroom whenever there's a bathroom handy.

She bought you a toe ring when she went to Mexico on vacation.

She still can't figure out how to open up your saved E-mail file.

Mom keeps fresh cherries in her fridge at least eight months of the year.

Mothers know which battles
are worth fighting.

Mothers know where to buy
Hanro underwear at a discount.

She loves cruises. One day,
she'll even take you on one.

Great Moms in Literature

Mrs. Portnoy

～

Medea

～

Clytemnestra

Mother Courage

Mrs. Bennett

Mrs. Cottontail

Ma in the *Little House* books

Mrs. Belden in the
Trixie Belden mysteries

"Jules" Ray in the Betsy-Tacy books

Marmee

Mrs. Robin (Christopher's mom)

The wolf who suckled
Romulus and Remus

Mama in *Mama's Bank Account*

Jean Kerr
(in *Please Don't Eat the Daisies*)

She talks to her friends about wanting to go on a spiritual journey to Machu Picchu, but you know she'd rather shoot craps in Las Vegas.

Moms believe in dessert.

And one for good luck.

She makes it all look sooo easy.

When no one asked you to dance
at the Christmas party, your
mother was even sadder
than you.

She takes the time to use shoe trees.

Moms always have enough
quilted hangers.

Remember that time she got
tickets for *The Producers* and she
couldn't go because she had to
take you to the emergency room?

A mother might give you a little
tiny sip of her wine on holidays.

When you're sick in bed,
she'll let you watch horrible
soap operas and infomercials.

Mothers are not afraid to
unclog a toilet.

Mothers know the running stitch
and the backstitch.

You can always borrow her
glue gun.

Bad Moms
in Literature

Mrs. Portnoy

Medea

Eve

Cinderella's stepmother

Snow White's stepmother

Hansel and Gretel's stepmother

Mrs. Lenox in *The Secret Garden*

Madame Bovary

Amanda in *The Glass Menagerie*

Hera

Nicole Diver

Gertrude

Mrs. Capulet

Hester Prynne

Norman Bates's mother

Scarlett O'Hara

Aren't there some things you're
secretly relieved your mother
is strict about?

On holidays, she uses
a tablecloth . . .

. . . And remembers to get
it cleaned before that
wine stain sets.

All those nights she spent
rocking you when you had an
ear infection . . .

She empties the dehumidifier
before it floods.

Only a mother can turn a
dead-of-winter power outage
into a "Cozy Campout."

She doesn't expect you to name the baby "Eudora Suzeen" after her.

Somehow, mothers always know when it's time to start getting a rinse.

She's been planning your wedding since the day you were born.

Mothers always have a spare
Chap Stick up their sleeve.

She has a secret, interesting past
that you will never hear about.

And she is much more aware of
your secret, interesting past than
you realize.

They believe in the power
of elbow grease.

If a mother impulse-buys a rabbit,
she will take care of it herself.

Mothers know the difference
between a broth and a consommé.

And the difference between
damask and chintz.

And the difference between
vinyl and Naugahyde.

And the difference between
a house and a home.

And the difference between
a romantic and a stalker.

And the difference between
a rock and a hard place.

Great Things to Say to Your Mom

More broccoli, please.

Would it be okay if I went
to bed early tonight?

I'd like a nice conservative
party dress this year.

You're the skinniest mother in the whole Brownie troop.

We had a vote and it was unanimous: You're the best mom!

You are right—that T-shirt I've been wearing for ten years *is* ready for the garbage.

How do you think I should
do my hair?

Do you think this length
is right for me?

I walked the dog.

I emptied the litter box.

It stands for Designated Driver.
They call me that because
I never drink.

They only picked ten kids
in the whole country and we get
to meet the President.

One hundred percent financial aid.

They made us write an essay on
our most influential person,
and I picked you.

No, tell me the truth. If you
don't like him, I'll break up
immediately.

We're naming her after you.

Jason's dad thought you
were my sister!

Will you be in the labor room
with me? Ted's afraid he'll faint.

And this will be your wing . . . with its own entrance, of course.

Can I empty the dishwasher?

It's like you always said, Mom . . .

Not-So-Great Things to Say to Your Mom

I'm not sure when I'll be home.

I forget his last name.

He doesn't live with his parents anymore.

I didn't think he assigned us
any homework.

Didn't you say I could
borrow the car?

A couple of little things happened
to the car when I borrowed it.

What's wrong with tattoos?

It followed me home.

I didn't bother making my bed at Peter's house. His mom can do it.

I only invited about fifteen kids over this weekend!

She's not a delinquent; she's misunderstood.

I'd like to take some time off.

I signed you up to play basketball
on the parents' team.

Who cares about Yale?

Some Jehovah's Witnesses came to
the door. I told them to come
back when you'll be home.

I want to act.

You don't mind if I shave my hair off, do you?

Her parents won't be at home.

Mrs. Kolody looks way younger than you.

That cute math teacher wants me to stay after for special coaching.

When I was taking some money out of your purse, I found that note that guy sent you.

My cell phone won't work there.

I've always had the feeling you
wish I'd been a son.

It only *looks* cleaned up. I shoved
all my toys under the bed.

It's easier to put my clothes
in the laundry hamper than
to hang them up.

She remembers to feed your
hermit crabs even though she
hates their scrabbly little legs.

A mother would never take
such a long shower that all the
hot water ran out.

Or forget to turn off the
bathtub faucet and flood the
living room underneath.

Moms are great at picking
you out of a crowd . . .

. . . Even in a camp photo
where you're hidden behind
three hundred other girls in
identical uniforms.

She has her original
Nutcracker Suite tutu, and it's
yours for the taking.

Moms know extra verses of "Miss Mary Mack" and the unexpurgated "Miss Lucy Had a Steamboat" clapping games.

Likewise, new (old) versions of hopscotch and jacks.

Ask your mother to curtsy, and you'll roll over laughing.

She's from the last generation
that still polishes its shoes.

When Mom finds a web site
that still sells Beeman's gum, she
orders you a whole case.

Boy, can she jitterbug!

Great Things About Mothers-to-Be

You don't have to
wear sunscreen in utero.

They talk to you even though
you're not listening.

They quit drinking
for *your* health.

They provide you with free transportation, food, and medical care.

Help yourself to all the calcium you can extract!

They think it's cute when you kick them.

They don't criticize your haircut.

They don't notice when
you wake up early.

They put your sonogram picture
on the refrigerator.

It's always nice and warm in there.

They put headphones on
their stomachs so you can hear
(and ignore) Mozart.

They don't resent you for
making them fat.

They won't forget to pick you up
when it's delivery time.

When you're older, she'll tell you
the story of the Christmas party
when she met the senator.

Moms buy paper doilies
for you to color.

Hearing your mother swear, you
feel like the East Germans did when
the Berlin Wall came down.

When she says, "I love you,"
it still makes you beam.

She knows what Isabelle's mother
will say if you don't save a seat
for her on the class trip.

Luckily, she changed her mind
about naming you "Solstice."

She wouldn't be a bit surprised
if you wound up as president.

At the beginning of a new school
year, she never makes you use
leftover school supplies
from last June.

Mothers always say you look
great in your new glasses.

She doesn't waste time on
sightseeing in Rome;
she shops all day without guilt.

Mothers cry the first time the
school bus takes you away.

Mom knows how to preserve
fall leaves by ironing them
between sheets of waxed paper.

Great Things About Moms Whatever Your Age

One minute old:
The one time in your life they
won't blame you for all the trouble
you put them through.

One hour old:
They've already used up
sixty rolls of film on you.

One day old:
They won't ask you to take out
the garbage or set the table.

Two days old:
By now, they can actually pick
you out of the other babies
in the hospital nursery.

Three days old:
Milk's in! Help yourself.

Five days old:
They call the pediatrician at the
drop of a hat.

Eight days old:
They feel a lot worse about your
circumcision than you do.

Ten days old:
If they drink a little wine while
nursing, you'll get your first buzz.

Two weeks old:
They don't expect you to be "on a schedule" yet.

Four weeks old:
Man, they go *crazy* when you smile at them. Such a big result for such a small effort.

Six weeks old:
They feel self-conscious about your "infant acne," even though you don't.

Two months old:
They're proud of your infant
poops.

Three months old:
They stop lugging you around in
that hot, uncomfortable Snugli.

Five months old:
They don't mind expressing their
milk for you, even if they have to
pump at the law firm.

Six months old:
They think you're sitting up when you're actually falling over.

Seven months old:
They think you're standing when you're actually just propped up against the coffee table.

Eight months old:
At this point, they *like* the fact that you can crawl everywhere.

Nine months old:
They always have an extra jar of
strained pears.

One year old:
At this point, they *like* the fact that
you can walk everywhere.

Eighteen months old:
mmmmm, cuddling with Mommy.

Two years old:
They write off the most intolerable
behavior as the "terrible twos."

Three years old:
As if you would have enjoyed
toilet-training yourself . . .

Four years old:
She thinks your drawing of
Grandpa looks like a Picasso.

Five years old:
They actually cry harder than you
do on your first day of
kindergarten.

Six years old:
She'll help you sound out words
without getting impatient.

Seven years old:
She thinks it's sweet that you're the
last person in your class who still
believes in Santa Claus.

Eight years old:
She won't tell your teacher that you
didn't practice piano this week.

Nine years old:
She'll quiz you on your
vocabulary words.

Ten years old:
She makes such a big deal out of
your being a "double digit" now.

Eleven years old:
A gift just because you have to
wear head gear!

Twelve years old:
Even though Ruby is your dog,
she'll clean up the mess.

Thirteen years old:
She bought you a formal dress to
wear to the bar mitzvah even
though she knew you'd never
wear it again.

Fourteen years old:
Okay, you can get your
belly-button pierced.

Fifteen years old:
You're going through an ugly
phase, but she doesn't think so.

Sixteen years old:
It's funny to watch her slam her
foot down on an imaginary brake
when she's teaching you to drive.

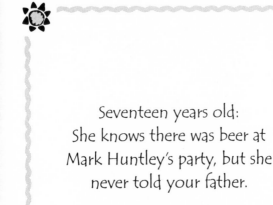

Seventeen years old:
She knows there was beer at
Mark Huntley's party, but she
never told your father.

Eighteen years old:
Don't worry, she'll get you
to the SATs on time.

After what you put her through,
she's earned the right to take it easy.

Sometimes she watches schlocky
TV when you're at school.

Mothers are never embarrassed
to be in a book group.

They always lift things to
vacuum under them.

Mothers can tell you who the people in old family photos are.

She'll drop everything in order to play Crazy Eights for hours when you have strep throat.

She went to college with Blythe Danner. When you were a baby, you used to play in the sandbox with Gwyneth Paltrow.

Mom knows all the lyrics to
"Sympathy for the Devil."

She gave you a brother.

A mother will carry your winter
coat all day in an overheated
department store or museum.

In an emergency—an emergency,
young lady—she will lend you
her credit card.

She's not offended when you
pour ketchup all over the dinner
she makes for you.

You get her religion.

She taught you all about
moisturizing before it was too late.

She'll always put sunscreen
all over your body before she
protects herself from the sun.

Moms braid your hair in the
morning before school.

She loves Daddy.

She knows every single episode of
The Mary Tyler Moore Show by
heart, and can recite dialogue while
you're watching it on Nick at Nite.

Garth Brooks once invited her
to go rowing with him.

She can poach a salmon, grill a
lamb chop, and bake a loaf of
bread without fanfare.

You can color each other's hair.

Mothers come to the play
you're in, no matter how early
in the morning it starts.

Mom keeps the myth of
Santa Claus alive.

She's personally acquainted with
the Easter bunny as well.

The Top Mom Tips of All Time

I don't care how much you like him—girls shouldn't call boys.

If you can't say anything nice, don't say anything at all.

Think of it as an adventure!

Watch other people if you're not sure which fork to use.

Cooking rice—water's twice.

If you roll up your T-shirts and sweaters, you can get more into your suitcase.

Just before you go out at night,
take off one piece of jewelry.
(You probably had on too much.)

Who will buy the cow
if the milk is free?

It's as easy to fall in love
with a rich man as a poor one.

No one's going to notice your thighs, silly, you have such a beautiful smile.

Don't fill up on bread.

There are other fish in the sea.

Don't go out with a wet head.

Under no circumstances
may you run with a pair of scissors
in your hand!

You cannot have a fifth piercing.

Engraved stationery is a
sensible investment.

I'm not insisting that you
major in economics; I'm just
asking you to take one course.

Call your stepfather and wish him
happy birthday.

Always shop for shoes
in the afternoon, when your
feet are bigger.

When in doubt, throw it out.

Clean walls from the top down,
or the bottom up, or whatever.

Don't drench yourself in perfume.

Always do your homework
before supper.

Don't suck in your stomach
when you're measuring your waist.

Never stare at the sun.

Hot pan, cold oil.

Brush your teeth in little circles,
not side to side.

The milk cartons in the back
are fresher.

You can part your hair with a pencil
if you don't have a comb.

Never discuss politics or religion
with someone you don't know.

If you're making someone
a casserole, bake it in a foil pan
they can throw away.

Don't drink the water.

She remembers to get your teachers
end-of-the-year presents.

She always sides with you, even
when your husband is right.

She carries your picture
in her wallet.

She'll decide when you're ready
for a bra.

She never ever forgets
your phone number.

Never forgets your birthday,
either.

She makes sure you're up and
at 'em on school days.

Who else hangs your artwork?

She remembers what size you are.

She actually likes that macaroni collage you made for Mother's Day.

The "Facts of Life" lecture embarrasses her as much as you.

She'll never admit that she likes you better than your sister or brother . . . but she does.

She knows that the best Easter egg dyes are the Ukranian ones at the craft store.

She's not embarrassed to take Aquacise classes.

Maternal instinct means always giving you the last piece of pie.

She'll buy your class picture
even if your eyes are shut.

She'll spoil your children.

At the nadir of your ugly phase,
she still thinks you're cute.

You made her throw up and
gain weight for nine months,
but she still loves you.

If you ever need a kidney,
she's a possible match.

Your homework is her homework.

If you say pretty please, she might
buy Oreo cookies next time she
goes grocery shopping.

Name one person who didn't
have a mother!

Great Mother's Day Presents

Dinner at the best restaurant
in town.

Those hand-in-clay molds.

A collection of recipes written by everyone in the first grade.

A maid service.

A window-washing service.

Cleaning out the basement
or garage.

A promise to weed the borders
all summer long.

A donation in Mom's name
to a charity.

OnStar.

You've got to admit: When they
get dressed up, Mom and Dad are
a pretty snazzy couple.

She probably won't disgrace you
at the PTA meeting.

She's an expert hair braider.

A.k.a. the Tooth Fairy.

She yells at you to pick up your
toys, then picks them up herself.

She'll baby-sit your children and
clean your house at the same time.

When she moves into a smaller
place, her dining room set is yours.

She's better than Brenda's mom.

Send those college tuition bills
to Mom's house!

Mothers let you take money out
of their wallets.

They let you rifle through their
pocketbooks, too.

They give you keys to the house
without thinking twice.

Mom knows why Aunt Barb walked
out on Uncle Larry—and when
you're a little older, she'll tell you.

Your mother's fashion sense
is perfect . . .

. . . Until you reach the
seventh grade.

She knows how to talk to the tailor.

Your mother would never
stand you up.

Mommy-spit on a tissue is just as
good as soap on a washcloth.

Moms aren't embarrassed about
singing to their kids . . .

. . . Even when, in the kids'
opinion, they should be.

She can load that dishwasher fuller than anyone else on the planet.

She's not afraid to smash a wasp in a paper towel.

Moms can clean up vomit without (overtly) gagging.

Mothers' lipsticks have exotic names like Coral and Melon.

She carries a pad and paper in
her purse for when you get
bored at church.

That nice smell of face powder.

She lets you keep mealworms for
your hedgehog in the refrigerator.

Who else can teach you to make
a hospital corner?

Not-So-Great Mother's Day Presents

Breakfast in bed.

Cardboard bookends.

Cleaning supplies.

Your old running shoes, bronzed.

Drugstore cologne
(unless the giver is under
ten years old).

One more potted plant.

A phone call in which
you ask for money.

She'll bring up your lunch on a tray when you get sick.

She may even put a bell on the tray for you to ring if you need her.

Moms know how to use a cake-decorating tube.

They don't mind reading *The Runaway Bunny* over and over.

They keep crackers in the glove
compartment in case you're
starving after piano lessons.

She'll write you lots of letters
at camp . . .

. . . But she won't come and take
you home early, no matter
how homesick you are.
(Camp builds character.)

A mother always has a Kleenex
up her sleeve.

Mothers are great at coming up
with paying chores if you really
need money.

You never knew she could
do cartwheels!

Her old bridesmaids' dresses
make great costumes.

The primitive toys from
her childhood are
endlessly fascinating.

She's the only one who
remembers where your
old Barbies are.

She's the only one who
remembers where your old
high school diploma is.

She's too nice to throw away any
of your old schoolwork . . .

. . . And will give it to you so that
you can throw it away.

She's not ashamed to pray in front of other people.

She comes to all your field-hockey games . . .

. . . And then stops coming when you tell her you play worse with her around.

A Mother's Supernatural Powers

She can read your mind and
know when you hit your sister.

She can see through bedroom walls
to check when you're asleep.

She can pick up cigarettes on your
breath even after you've used
a gallon of mouthwash.

At the school concert, she can
spot you all the way in the
back row behind Marlene Heiklen.

She hears a baby crying
a million miles away.

She can tell the Discman's on
too high even though all
she can hear is the bass.

She can hear a baby's pacifier
fall out of its mouth from
another room. Down the hall.
Without a baby monitor.

She knows you're throwing
a party at home even though
she's in Bermuda.

She knows you don't have a fever
just by looking at you.

She can tell by the way you say
"hi" that you didn't get elected
class president.

She knows what a
dolman sleeve is.

She knows what ruching is.

She knows what
trapunto stitching is.

She doesn't have to turn around
to know that you have
"that expression" on your face.

She knows when you have lots
of homework that you're
not doing.

She can smell liquor on your breath
before you're even in the house.

She travels faster than the
speed of light to push a baby's hand
away from the stove.

At least she *tries* to help with
your math homework.

Mothers are brave about
getting cabs.

Car pools, car pools, car pools.

Diapers, diapers, diapers.

Her pot roast.

Her mashed potatoes.

She can show you how to
turn a somersault.

And how to tease your hair.

All mothers who are alive today
love the Beatles.

A mom will let you quit almost
any activity if you tell her it's
interfering with your schoolwork.

Think of all the morning sickness
they put up with to get you.

She knows the most outlandish
jump-rope rhymes.

Even though their babies don't
come with owners' manuals,
mothers somehow figure it out.

It was nice of her to come on
the class field trip to the
post office, even though you
didn't want her to.

She saves one pan just for omelettes.

She doesn't say "I told you so" nearly as often as she could.

A good mother pays for her adult child's therapy.

All mothers are determined to do a better job than their mothers did.

She lets you drink coffee even though she really *is* afraid it will stunt your growth.

Remember when she took up the double bass because your school orchestra needed one?

She knows just what to cook to make the house smell good on a cold winter day.

Great Quotes About Moms

"God could not be everywhere,
and therefore he made mothers."
—Jewish proverb

"The hand that rocks the cradle is
the hand that rules the world."
—W. S. Ross

"A mother is not a person
to lean on, but a person
to make leaning unnecessary."
—Dorothy Canfield Fisher

"All that I am, or hope to be,
I owe to my angel mother."
—Abraham Lincoln

"The mother's heart
is the child's schoolroom."
—Henry Ward Beecher

"As is the mother,
so is her daughter."
—Ezekiel 1:16

"Despise not thy mother
when she is old."
—Proverbs 23:22

"A man who has been the
indisputable favorite of his
mother keeps for life the feeling
of a conqueror."
—Ernest Jones

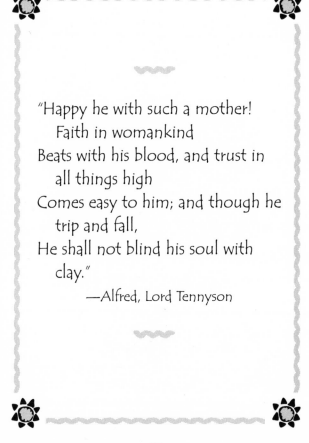

"Happy he with such a mother!
Faith in womankind
Beats with his blood, and trust in
all things high
Comes easy to him; and though he
trip and fall,
He shall not blind his soul with
clay."

—Alfred, Lord Tennyson

"Who ran to help me when I fell,
And would some pretty story tell,
Or kiss the place to make it well?
My mother."
—Jane Taylor

"If I were damned of body and
  soul,
I know whose prayers would make
  me whole,
Mother o' mine, O mother o' mine!"
—Rudyard Kipling

"She's somebody's mother, boys,
you know,
For all she's aged and poor and
slow."
—Mary Dow Brine

"I cannot bear a mother's tears."
—Virgil

"Sons are the anchors
of a mother's life."
—Sophocles

Mom will put on your Band-Aid.

And kiss the place where you
got your boo-boo.

You can easily distract her by asking
questions about her childhood.

She'll make whatever you want for
your birthday dinner.

Mothers are even more embarrassed than you when they catch you making out with your boyfriend.

They'll check to make sure there are no monsters under the bed or in the closet.

Mothers' sunglasses are so ugly that you're never tempted to borrow them.

They always let you get your
ears pierced earlier than they
thought they would.

If you're sick, your mom will
take a sick day herself to stay
home with you.

She won't sue if you write a
mean memoir about her.

She worries that your best friend
isn't getting enough attention
at home.

For some reason, many moms
know how to tie a four-in-hand.

Mothers will let their teens sleep
until five in the afternoon.

It's hilarious when a mom burps.

If you're a vegetarian, she'll cook
a separate meal for you . . .

. . . But if you're a meat-eater
and she's a vegetarian, you're
on your own.

"Man works from sun to
setting sun, but woman's work
is never done."

She got Lasik before you did.

Remember when she helped you make that Father's Day plaque? You never did get around to making a Mother's Day plaque . . .

You always know when she's lying.

And vice versa.

Mothers don't keep their favorite recipes a secret from their children.

Moms never tell their daughters how horrible labor really is.

She makes sure to keep you properly hydrated.

Mothers are the only ones who keep track of the overdue videos.

They rarely refuse to take their kids to the emergency room.

At Thanksgiving, Mom reminds you about those who are less fortunate than you.

On balance, her lack of vanity is probably a good thing.

"I Wish I Had a Mother Who . . ."

. . . Wore pearly eyeshadow.

. . . Knew Mary Kate and Ashley Olsen.

. . . Let me stay out past 1:00 A.M.

. . . Didn't walk so near me
in public places.

. . . Slept like a log.

. . . Didn't talk to my friends when
she's driving us somewhere.

. . . Had really nice handwriting.

. . . Drove a cool car.

. . . Didn't fumble for the exact change in the supermarket line.

. . . Didn't sing along to the radio.

. . . Gave me money for my birthday instead of presents.

. . . Didn't peek into the middle-school gym when she came to pick me up at the dance.

. . . Didn't accidentally call me by my brother's name.

. . . Didn't accidentally call me by my dog's name.

. . . Hadn't taken pictures of me in the bathtub when I was a baby.

. . . Would throw out those ugly Christmas ornaments I made in preschool.

. . . Would stay upstairs the whole time when I have a party.

She can get a kid into a snowsuit
in ten seconds flat.

She can get a kid out of a
snowsuit in five seconds flat when
the kid announces that he has
to go to the bathroom.

Mothers are good at tightening
your skates.

They all come with a recipe
for play dough.

She can show you what to do
at the Communion rail.

It's not cheating if *she* helps you
write your paper.

She understands that you can't give
up your blankie yet.

She understands that you're not
ready to quit sucking your thumb.

If she helps you with the cover
of your report, it's not the same as
doing the report, and besides,
she won't let you use an
Exacto knife anyway.

When you were so scared of that
Hansel and Gretel tape, she pulled
it all out and threw it away
while you watched.

Remember when she got
those mail-order steaks and let you
play with the dry ice they
came packed in?

She picks the best goodie bags
for birthday parties!

Mom was right, after all, when
she wouldn't let you adopt
that spider monkey.

When you already have your
mittens on, she'll tie your hood
for you.

Only mothers can get all
the socks organized.

They're great at
taking out splinters.

Her iced tea is the best.

Mary must've been a pretty great
mother to Jesus.

She let you get that weird
wallpaper in seventh grade . . .

. . . And didn't yell when you
painted it over in eighth grade.

She'll let you have the cast party
at your house.

When you've moved away,
she'll send you newspaper clippings
about your friends who stayed
at home.

She has a huge cache of
blue-edge stoneware.

Hey, she's probably in
better shape than you are.

Special Mom Foods

Swiss steak

Baked hamburgers on toast

"Brunch casserole"

Beef Stroganoff

Carrot sticks

Tomato soup with
oyster crackers

Meat loaf

Apple wedges

Orange quarters

Potato salad

Grilled cheese

Cambric tea

"Overnight French Toast"

Milkshakes
with an egg in them

Chicken Country Captain

Swedish meatballs

Oven-fried chicken

Peanut butter
and bacon sandwiches

Russian tea cakes

"Store candy" smuggled into
the movies to save money

She got up every two hours to feed
that abandoned baby bird.

You'll inherit all her Chanel suits.

She gets the last dregs out of
the shampoo bottle by filling
it with water.

Mom still uses that spoon rest
you made in pottery class.

She went without a new
winter coat for eleven years.

She can get the snarls out
without hurting you.

She still has her old record player
and a big stack of 45s.

She cares, really cares, whether you
try the tandoori chicken.

She cares, really cares, whether
you wipe your feet before
you come in.

Look, mothers aren't *trying*
to embarrass us.

She took you to that children's
playwriting conference the day
after her face-lift.

Mom's
Ten Commandments

Sick people belong in bed.

Thank-you notes, thank-you notes, thank-you notes.

Everyone needs a nap every day.

Get your hair off your face.

Stand up straight.

Look people in the eye
when you meet them.

Good table manners are important
in case you get invited to a
rich person's house for dinner.

If you get a pet, I'll end up
taking care of it.

You can't go outside in that.

Whatever you're doing, stop it.

Your mother will let you try on
her engagement ring.

She dreads chaperoning your
dancing-school classes even more
than you dread having her there.

In a pinch, her sister can
substitute for her.

Mothers can reach the top shelf.

What's in Mom's Purse?

Button that fell off her brown coat

Recipe for chocolate bread

Two-day-old newspaper crossword

Three pens that don't work

Puzzle piece from a puzzle
she threw out

Dog biscuit for luring away
a strange dog

An old Cracker Jack prize

Enough Kleenex shreds
to make a new Kleenex

Leaking perfume sample
from the Saks counter

Barbie shoe

Glitter from Valentine
you made for her

Chap Stick

Little tin of aspirin (empty)

Book for her book club

Mints

Canadian coins

A golf tee, for some reason

She has a crush on Johnny Depp too!

(But she doesn't expect you to
share him with her.)

It really does hurt them to
say no to you.

If Dad's not there, your mother
has to read the subway map.

She saved Grandma's christening
dress all these years . . .

. . . Only to be told you're having
a Druid tree-planting ceremony
and not a christening.

She didn't faint that time you
cut your thumb open on the
soda can.

And she took the thumbtack out
of your heel like a pro.

She knows every single verse of
"I Know an Old Lady."

She won't tell you how
Gone with the Wind ends,
no matter how hard you beg her.

A mother always knows what kind of ties Dad likes.

As you get older, she will share her back-strengthening exercises with you.

No one else would cry over your performance of the nameless shepherd in the Christmas pageant.

Lies It's Okay for a Mother to Tell

Yes, it *is* midnight.
Now go to bed.

I never did anything like that
when I was a teenager.

That dress does not
make you look fat.

That dress makes you look fat.

A smile makes anyone
look beautiful.

These are the best years
of your life.

You'll have a great time.

No. I like dark meat best.

He only broke up with you
because he realized he wasn't
good enough for you.

I think it's a good haircut.

I won't say another word.

Of course married people
don't have affairs.

Of course married people

They don't have more money
than we do. They just spend
it differently.

I heard every word of your speech
loud and clear.

Thank you! It's exactly what
I wanted!

Daddy and I aren't fighting.
We're just discussing something.

I would never read your mail.

When I was your age,
I never did that.

We love all of you equally.

Of course we didn't sneak
downstairs and spy on your party.

Of course we didn't put a
baby monitor in the rec room
during your party.

Of course I don't swear.

The store was completely out of cookies.

You were the best in the play by far.

Bedtime in fifteen minutes.

She keeps track of all the
library books.

Come to think of it, Mom
was right—Michael Giordano
was wrong for you.

But if you had stayed with
Michael Giordano, she would
have coped.

She knows what to say
to telemarketers.

Once you've tasted your father's
scrambled eggs, you'll never
complain about your mother's
cooking again.

She'll go to the spa with you . . .
and pay for your stay.

Mothers always keep the picnic supplies organized.

They remember where you left your SAT information.

Let Mom deal with the bellboy.

She gave you a cool name because her own was so incredibly boring and banal.

Sure Signs of an Inexperienced Mom

Purees all her own baby food.

Sterilizes the pacifier whenever baby drops it.

Worries when toddler grabs another toddler's toy.

Worries that toddler wants
"too much exercise."

Expects child to be toilet-trained
before three.

Expects to get a full night's sleep
before child is ten.

Doesn't let girls have Barbies.

Doesn't let boys have toy guns.

Doesn't bring potty-seat in car.

Doesn't want child to get dirty.

Brings one picture book
to entertain child on
transatlantic flight.

Takes it personally when baby cries.

Worries that she won't have time
to put on her makeup before
going into labor.

Thinks her preschooler's test scores
will keep her out of Yale.

Rents *Jurassic Park* because her
two-year-old loves Barney.

Plans to bring up child bilingually,
though she herself does not speak
a second language.

Doesn't carry wipes with her
at all times.

Scared to "bother" the pediatrician
in an emergency.

Worries that toddler doesn't eat
enough vegetables.

Thinks it matters what kind
of stroller you get.

Expects that baby-proofing
the house will prevent
the unexpected.

It's cute the way mothers think a homemade juice pop is just as good as a Fudgsicle.

She never pinches your cheek the way Aunt Lucy does.

Mom will always tell you frankly, freely, and honestly that your new boots are grotesquely unflattering.

She vacuums the baseboards.

If she exercises, you're
more likely to as well.

Now that you have kids of
your own, you realize what she
went through.

Things Only a Mother Has

The Talbot's catalog

A subscription to *Bon Appétit*

Geraniums

Enough vases

Handi Wipes

Endust

A canning kettle

Sabbath candles

Clip-on earrings

Rockport walking shoes

A prayer book

Monogrammed stationery

Your old report cards

Chanel No. 22 dusting powder

Cheesecloth

A travel iron

Embroidery needles

A bathing cap

A shower cap

Her old bridesmaids' dresses

Corn-on-the-cob holders

A fondue set

A list of whom to send
Christmas cards to

Oil of Olay

Penny loafers

Madeleine pans

Paste

The Libman Wonder Mop

A hard-boiled-egg slicer

Slippers

A star chart recording your chores

A pincushion

A jar full of spare buttons

A bra-slip

If she's in the delivery room with
you, she won't try to distract you
with worthless Lamaze techniques.

If you happen to mention that you
need a couple of new wing chairs,
they just might appear!

However painful, she knows it's
her job to let you go . . .

You wouldn't do your own
Add-a-Pearl necklace.

She'll let you keep your
panty hose in the freezer when
you decide it keeps them
from getting runs so fast.

She'll write an excuse for you
when you really couldn't get
your homework done.

But she won't write an excuse when you could have gotten it done, because "it wouldn't be fair to you."

She always has an extra comb.

Moms have a special "telephone voice."

She knows what to say to
old people.

She didn't turn your bedroom
into a guest room until ten years
after you had left home.

If mothers don't nag us about
our table manners, who will?

Moms know where to buy big huge
bags of Popsicle sticks.

She'll never tell your dad about
the time you knocked the
mirror off that other car in
the parking lot.

She knows how long meat
can stay in the freezer.

Great Things Your Mother Says but May Not Believe

All I want is for you to be happy.

This is the only time I'll ask . . .

Of course you're prettier
than Tammy.

x

x

254

Money isn't as important
as manners.

This hurts me more than
it hurts you.

The most important thing is
that you do your best.

You'll thank me someday.

Grown-ups are just as cool as kids,
but in a different way.

I'm not saying no;
I'm saying I'll think about it.

The last thing you want is to
look like everyone else.

You'll understand when
you're older.

It would never occur to small
children to buy their own
Raffi tapes.

She knows the rules to
"Go Fish" and "Authors."

Her girdle is interesting, isn't it?

She let you take ballet even though
she knew nothing would come of it.

She paid for your braces even
though she knew you'd never wear
your retainer long enough.

At scary movies, you can hide
your eyes in Mom's coat.

Mom remembers that you hate
celery in your tuna salad.

Oh, the songs she's sung you . . .

A mother's brain can keep track
of all her kids' peanut-butter-and-
jelly-sandwich preferences.

Long after she's forgotten
everything else, she'll still smile
at the sight of your face.

She knows the location of every
public rest room in the city.

Mom-Crit

I'm just curious. Do all the girls in your grade dress like tramps?

~

We missed you so much this summer. Eight weeks is just too long. Now will you let me do something with your hair?

~

Do I smell smoke?

Here's an article from the
New York Times about how those
shoes can ruin your feet for life.

I'll give you a hundred dollars if
you let me throw out those jeans.

You're so beautiful. Why do you
have to hide it with those bangs?

What's that on your forehead?

It's beautiful the way your friend Caitlyn shakes hands and looks people right in the eye when she meets them.

Do you want me to put some makeup on that thing?

You know there's medicine now that takes care of that.

While you were gone, I cleaned all that crap out of your closets. Is that okay?

Hi. How was school? I've been thinking about it all day and I decided you need a navy blazer to pull everything together.

Stand up straight. You look like Uncle Peter.

I told you not to get a tattoo. Now don't come back until it's gone.

I don't like this gaunt look that you're trying to do now.

What a pretty dress. You really want to be wearing those shoes?

Is *that* the jacket you wore to your interview?

I have to pass along something
Mrs. Deane pointed out
about you . . .

I think you could use some
makeup . . . more makeup, then.

Don't take this the wrong way,
but were your eyebrows
always asymmetrical?

I don't know what you and
that hairdresser of yours think
you're doing.

I'm doing you a favor
by telling you this.

I don't mean to be nitpicking,
but that's all wrong.

You look . . . well, I prefer you
when you're gaunt.

When are you coming home?
You sound like you've
gained weight.

Come here and let me pull out
that gray hair. I'm not old enough
for you to have gray hair.

Show me what you're going to wear to my funeral so I can let you know whether it's appropriate.

If I don't tell you the truth, who will?

I know Mrs. Abernathy has twenty students' papers to correct, so even though she gave you an A, I found a few little things that were wrong with your essay, if you want to see them.

Moms are really good at scraping food off the baby's face and putting it back into her mouth.

If you have to spend the night in the hospital, she'll sleep in a chair next to your bed.

She remembered the gum for the airplane trip.

She's much better at picking out
your clothes than your dad is.

She will needlepoint some new
chair covers any time you ask.

She'll take you to R movies as long
as they're not too embarrassing for
the two of you to see together.

Her basic wardrobe is totally vintage chic!

She's willing to sacrifice her health to make you better.

She'll stick up for you in court.

Just ask. She'll tell you what to buy for her birthday.

Would you rather have
Lori's mother?!

She'd never miss Parents' Day.

Mothers hardly ever say,
"You stink."

Wedding planner.

Claims to prefer the middle seat
in the airplane.

On vacation, she remembers
to hang up the bathing suits so
they'll be dry the next time
you need them.

Moms always have an
emory board handy.

Mythical Moms

Zeus, you put that
thunderbolt down *right now*.

Diana, you put that bow
and arrow down *right now*.

Sit down, Venus! We don't
stand up in a moving seashell.

Believe it or not, Midas, there
are more important things
than money.

No going out to play until
you've cleaned up that stable,
Hercules.

Medusa, I don't even want to
look at you until you've done
something about your hair.

Put the fleece back where
you found it, Jason.

Mars, you're going to have to
control that temper of yours.

Echo! Stop repeating everything
your sister says!

Stay in the shallow end, Neptune.

Face forward, Orpheus.

Hades, you really should go out
and get some fresh air for a change.

Persephone, I've told you and
told you not to take food
from strangers!

I'm sure you can get that
boulder up the hill if you'll just
be patient, Sisyphus.

Pandora, stop poking your nose
into what doesn't concern you.

I don't care if Bacchus is a god.
He's not a fit companion for you.

Um, Oedipus? We have a little . . .
problem.

Her magazine subscriptions
are your magazine subscriptions.

Maybe you can get her to tell you
stories about the guys she dated
before Daddy.

She knows how to cut your toenails
without tickling.

She'll let you have a Band-Aid
on your scraped knee even if it's
not bleeding.

Your mother's initials are the
same as yours. Voilà! Your
vintage monogram.

Childbirth was the most
excruciating experience of her life,
and yet she never held it
against you.

In a pinch, a mother will
mother children not her own.

She taught her best friend how
to inhale, but she'd rather die
than teach you.

She'd be a surprisingly well-rounded
Lifeline for you on *Who Wants
to Be a Millionaire.*

She has some kind of NPR ESP:
She can find all the public radio
stations within moments of
arriving in a new place.

Her Phi Beta Kappa key will
make a wonderful charm for
your daughter one day.

Dislikes being called "Mom"
and allows you the sophisticated
privilege of calling her by
her first name.

Her family has been in the costume
business for three generations.

She never changes her
phone number.

Your name is her secret password
at the ATM.

And she told you so.

She takes good care of her car.

She hates Martha Stewart
more than you do.

She lets you sleep in her bed
when you're scared.

And even massages your back
when you don't ask her to.

She taught you how to hold
your breath underwater.

She knows her doilies from
her antimacassars.

She named you for her
favorite character in a
Rumer Godden book.

And didn't mind when you
changed your name in the
eleventh grade.

She went with you
to the tattoo parlor.

She says if she were growing up
now, she'd have lived with Dad
before getting married to him.

You'll get free decorating advice when
you get your first apartment . . .

. . . And free gardening advice
when you have your first yard.

Moms never forget to put out
the guest towels.

She's good at making store-bought
stuffing taste homemade.

The Best Moms on TV

June Lockhart, Lassie's
(no, Timmy's) mom

Jane Wyatt,
Father Knows Best

Donna Reed,
The Donna Reed Show

Harriet Nelson,
*The Adventures of
Ozzie and Harriet*

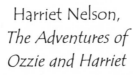

Shirley Jones,
The Partridge Family

Florence Henderson,
The Brady Bunch

Phylicia Rashad,
The Cosby Show

Katey Sagal,
Married . . . with Children

Barbara Billingsley,
Leave It to Beaver

Jane Kaczmarek,
Malcolm in the Middle

Pat Loud,
An American Family

Marge Simpson,
The Simpsons

Candice Bergen,
Murphy Brown

Jane Jetson,
The Jetsons

Wilma Flintstone,
The Flintstones

Nancy Marchand,
The Sopranos

Renee Taylor,
The Nanny

My Mother the Car
(the voice of Ann Sothern)

She's an automatic referee
during your boxing matches
with your siblings.

She knows what "darts" in a dress are.

She pretends to like raking leaves.

And doesn't yell when you
jump into the pile of leaves she's
just finished raking.

She knows which occasions are
appropriate for white gloves.

Mother-daughter dresses? She's in.

If you didn't have a mother,
you'd have nothing to talk about
at the shrink.

She thinks babies are boring, but
she thought *you* were fascinating.

She'd never open mail addressed
to you . . .

. . . But if she did, she'd reseal it
so you'd never know.

If the movie rating system didn't
exist, a mom would invent it.

She knows where the
adhesive tape is.

She knows where the coriander is
(and what it is).

She does all your ironing,
even when you're forty-four.

With all she had to do, she still
made sure you had a layette when
you came home from the hospital.

"This hurts me more than
it hurts you."

She'll never let you go outside
without sunscreen.

Only mothers know what
witch hazel is.

Can you believe that movies
only cost five dollars when she
was your age?!

Her expertise in folding.

Mothers are not embarrassed to
buy underwear for you.

Mothers understand when you say,
"Please don't look like you
recognize me in public."

When she picks you up at a
birthday party, she thanks the
hostess—which reminds you to
say thank you too.

Mom will take the garter snake out
of the swimming-pool filter.

She's so sentimental about your getting older that she cries when Hallmark has a graduation-card commercial on TV.

Once a mom, always a mom.